Endorsements

"*The Village Boy* is a book written about a young village boy and his appointment with destiny. The devil planned his death when his mother was six months' pregnant, but God had plans for him.

"This is the story of a village boy with grace, which has put on hold natural laws, caused protocols to be suspended, and formalities have been waived for his sake. Grace has continued to speak for this village boy, now a man.

"The author has used this book to express himself from his early childhood, his education, challenges, realities, a turning point, and Christian faith, as well as lessons for other people. The book is grouped into twenty parts from the village shepherd boy. My inspiration is in chapter one to the last chapter.

"The book cited several inspirational biblical quotations from the New King James Version. Indeed, the author used Psalm 103 to herald this book which is the watchword of the village boy.

"In preparing this book, the author has combined simplicity with depth and details with tens of scriptural references. The book is aimed at providing a concise and factual account of a village boy who has an appointment with destiny. The author has brought his Christian Apostolic calling and academic training to bear in his approach and presentation of the chapters of this work. He has admirably put this work together in lucid professional language with great care and respect for all readers to the extent the general public will benefit from it, especially those who want to be inspired to carry grace that has the capacity to suspend protocols and natural laws.

"This book is suitable for self-instruction as a companion to all. This is a must read for both old and young, especially those who need to be inspired to greater heights. It is recommended for students who want to have insight to the road to success. It is also a must to have in the family library."

Prof. B. E. B. Nwoke
Fellow, Academy of Science,
Department of Animal and Environmental Biology
Imo State University Owerri Nigeria

"It has been my pleasure to know Reverend Williams Ebiringa since 2008 in a friendship that has gone from mere acquaintance to partnership in ministry. Ever since getting acquainted with him, I have watched him grow in his relationship with the Man Christ Jesus to the place where his heart burns with the desire to go deeper and deeper in the knowledge of the beauty of the Lord. I have watched his children become established as godly young people and have appreciated deeply the contributions this family has brought to this city, first to African Christian Fellowship (ACF), Washington, D.C., and now to the entire Christian community. His devotion to the work of the Lord is a source of inspiration to me."

Emmanuel Ekwo

"The Reverend Williams Ebiringa is a man of remarkable integrity and excellent leadership. It is obvious that his humble beginning and wealth of life experiences that resulted from challenges and adversities, have helped to shape him into a humble and caring Christian leader that he is. Without a doubt, being born and raised as a village boy, as Reverend Ebiringa has carefully articulated in this book, has endowed him with the complimentary qualities of diligence, determination, and focus, as evidenced in his life and the impact that he is making in the lives of others. Being born in a poor Nigerian village has neither hindered nor denied him of his God-ordained destiny. On the contrary, those challenging experiences were employed by God to produce a tested and proven leader in Reverend Ebiringa."

Rev. Dr. George Bassey Sr.,
Senior Pastor, National Wesleyan Church, Maryland, USA

"Reverend Williams Ebiringa has inscribed by the inspiration of the Holy Spirit a book that every Christian and leader in the local church must read. *The Village Boy* is not just a memoir but a spiritual nugget for people who desire a higher walk with God and have insatiable thirst for the Holy Spirit and the manifestation of His gifts in their lives. It also lays out principles of a simple and humble walk of faith in Jesus Christ and the gospel."

Bishop Okon Aquaowo

The Village Boy

Trusting God to Place Us Where We Belong

Williams Okwuchi Ebiringa

HIGHERLIFE
PUBLISHING & MARKETING

Published by HigherLife Publishing & Marketing
PO Box 623307
Oviedo, Florida 32762
www.ahigherlife.com

ISBN: 978-1-958211-52-6

LOC: 1-12808563150

Printed in the United States of America
10 9 8 7 6 5 4 3 2 1

Contents

Acknowledgments

I greatly appreciate the help of a co-laborer in the Lord's vineyard, Brother Promise Nnakwe, for his spiritual contribution to make this work a reality. Additionally, I thank my son-in-law, Mr. Sam Emeka Uwahemo Jr., for his good heart in assisting me in typing my manuscript. Thank you both so much.

Rev. Williams Okwuchi Ebiringa

Introduction

The Village Shepherd Boy: My Inspiration

Bless the Lord, O my soul; and all that is within me, bless His holy name!
Bless the Lord, O my soul, and forget not all His benefits:
Who forgives all your iniquities, who heals all your diseases,
Who redeems your life from destruction,
Who crowns you with lovingkindness and tender mercies,
Who satisfies your mouth with good things,

So that your youth is renewed like the eagle's.

The Lord executes righteousness and justice for all who are oppressed.
He made known His ways to Moses, His acts to the children of Israel.
The Lord is merciful and gracious, slow to anger, and abounding in mercy.
He will not always strive with us, nor will He keep His anger forever.
He has not dealt with us according to our sins,

Nor punished us according to our iniquities.

For as the heavens are high above the earth,

So great is His mercy toward those who fear Him;
As far as the east is from the west, so far has He removed our

transgressions from us.
As a father pities his children, so the Lord pities those who fear Him.
For He knows our frame; He remembers that we are dust.

As for man, his days are like grass; as a flower of the field, so he flourishes.
For the wind passes over it, and it is gone, and its place remembers it no more.
But the mercy of the Lord is from everlasting to everlasting on those who fear Him,
And His righteousness to children's children, to such as keep His covenant,
And to those who remember His commandments to do them.

The Lord has established His throne in heaven, and His kingdom rules over all.

Bless the Lord, you His angels, who excel in strength, who do His word,
Heeding the voice of His word.
Bless the Lord, all you His hosts, you ministers of His, who do His pleasure.
Bless the Lord, all His works, in all places of His dominion.

Bless the Lord, O my soul!

(Psalm 103 NKJV)

Psalm 103 is inspiring song was written by King David who was once a shepherd boy, and is the watchword of the village boy.

David was shepherded by God Himself in a small village called Bethlehem in the hill country of Judah. Bethlehem was later called "the city of David" because David made it his capital. David, the youngest son of Jesse of the tribe of Judah, was the embodiment of humility, passion, and care for others. He devoted his childhood to caring for his father's flock. In his passionate desire to protect them in that time, he fought a lion and a bear and killed them both to save the lives of the sheep. Little did he know that God was training him to deliver his own people from the hands of their enemies and a giant called Goliath. God still does mighty works with us today.

David was called "a man after God's own heart."

Chapter One

A Man after God's Own Heart

But now your kingdom shall not continue. The Lord has sought for Himself a man after His own heart, and the Lord has commanded him to be commander over His people, because you have not kept what the Lord commanded you.

(The prophet Samuel said this to King Saul in 1 Samuel 13:14 NKJV)

And when He had removed him, He raised up for them David as king, to whom also He gave testimony and said, "I have found David the son of Jesse, a man after My own heart, who will do all My will."

(Acts 13:22 NKJV)

David, the second king of Israel, was consumed with his relationship with the God of heaven. He discovered something God loved: God actually inhabits the praise of His people (Psa. 22:3). The NKJV says: "But you are holy, enthroned in the praises of Israel."

David became a musician, a psalmist, and a poet. We feel God's love and affection most keenly when we are focused on His will and have devoted ourselves fully to His praise and purpose for our lives. We are instructed to abide in God, which means that we should live and move to worship His name.

When David completed his training as a shepherd, competent in his skills, God showcased him before the entire nation of Israel. David was moved to the next level. It is never good to jump in line. God's plan and God's timing are vital.

Therefore thus says the LORD GOD:

> *Behold, I lay in Zion a stone for a foundation, a tried stone, a precious cornerstone, a sure foundation; whoever believes will not act hastily.*
>
> (Isaiah 28:16 NKJV)

An obedient and faithful disciple models good leadership and does not act hastily, but waits for God's timing.

One day, a giant of the Philistines came to the valley of Elah with his people and challenged the people of Israel to a duel: their champion against Goliath, man against giant.[1] Goliath was a trained soldier who knew all the tactics and strategies of his weaponry. He was trained to win. He knew that he was stronger than any one man in Israel, so he trusted that challenging them one-on-one would ensure a Philistine victory.

David's seven brothers were also trained soldiers in King Saul's army. None of them could face or challenge Goliath, who came out daily to taunt and challenge the Israeli forces. David was sent to bring food to his brothers, and when he heard Goliath, he was not put off by him like everyone else was.

David was different. He didn't even know how to use a bow and arrow, but he still decided to confront Goliath when he heard him abuse and mock Jehovah, the mighty God that David knew and served. So, one day when Goliath said, "I defy

---

1   You can read the full story in 1 Samuel 17.

the armies of Israel this day; give me a man, that we may fight together" (1 Sam. 17:10 NKJV), David volunteered.

King Saul, to show benevolence to David who was willing to rescue Israel from their shame, tried to arm David with armor and weapons. However, David rejected them because they were too sophisticated and heavy for him.[2] David, relying on the power of God and, without even a bow, had killed a lion and a bear fighting for his father's sheep, and now he moved without hesitation with his sling and five stones to challenge Goliath. By the power of God, David boldly faced Goliath with his sling and struck Goliath on the forehead. The stone sunk deep into Goliath's forehead and he fell. David took Goliath's sword from its sheath and cut off Goliath's head. The Philistines ran away with the Israelites in pursuit. Their champion was dead. God had presented an unknown youth, a shepherd boy to both the people of Israel and the Philistines, as His chosen "hero."

Do not undermine what God can do. Do not listen to people, but be sensitive to hear God instead. In David's case, his own brothers had accused him of being proud and deceitful when he asked what the reward for standing up to Goliath was. Here he was considering challenging a giant, and they just wanted to know why he wasn't taking care of the sheep! David had to follow God instead of listening to them.[3]

As David returned from the slaughter of the Philistines, Abner took David and brought him before Saul.[4] From that day on, David, the village shepherd boy became Saul's commander of his army above his older brothers who had served

---

2   See 1 Samuel 17:38–39.
3   See 1 Samuel 17:24–29.
4   See 1 Samuel 17:57–58.

in the army long before David's encounter with Goliath. On that same day, Jonathan, King Saul's son, became David's best friend, and they were inseparable until death. When you are committed to God's given course, promotion looks for you and finds you at God's appointed time.[5]

One of the many lessons we learn from David's story is that we can trust God to promote us and place us where we belong. It is not necessary to bribe the way to promotion. When we bribe our way, we might make headway, but we also suffer loss because a bribe is a dishonest act. When God places us, He catapults us to a peak from which no one can pull us because God will anoint us above our fellows. And in God, we are placed just where we belong and retain our integrity, which is priceless.

---

5   See Psalm 75:6–7.

Chapter Two

The Miracle Child

Behold, I and the children whom the Lord hath given me are for signs and for wonders in Israel from the LORD of hosts, which dwelleth in mount Zion.

(Isaiah 8:18)

Before I formed thee in the belly I knew thee; and before thou camest forth out of the womb I sanctified thee, and I ordained thee a prophet unto the nations.

(Jeremiah 1:5)

These are both fascinating Scriptures. Consider this: your place of birth could be an advantage to your divine destiny. Incredible! Do not underrate or undermine where you came from. The day I was born was recorded in heaven. It was Saturday, February 28, 1953. God made it significant as the last day of the month of February, but the miracle began before that in the womb.

The devil planned my death when my mother was six months pregnant. My mother had an accident and was in a coma for six hours. But God, the Master of the Universe, the Author of Life, did not permit it because He had a good plan for me. "For I know the thoughts that I think toward you, saith the Lord, thoughts of peace, and not of evil, to give you an expected end" (Jer. 29:11).

At the age of four, I accompanied my immediate elder sister to the newly established Local Authority School (LAS), a government-run elementary-level school. Life in our village was primitive. The walls of the building were nothing but palm fronds. My first day of school was in January. (According to the school calendar, this was the first term of the year.) At 100 degrees Fahrenheit, it was like taking a bath in the sun. It was so very hot. The scorching effect compelled me to stay at home for two years until cement block walls were finally erected.

My second time there was different. I worked hard and was striving competitively with the other students. I vividly remember the day I came back from school at the end of the school year with my results. When my mother asked me what my position in the class was, I burst into tears because I was only in fourth position. Before I had always taken first or second position. Throughout my childhood, I worked hard and was very focused on doing well.

Our end-of-the-year special exhibition was always a time of celebration. It was at this time that we received a special lump of fish or meat if we did well, which was rewarded according to our merit. The recipients of these awards for excellence had to have stellar grades—ranging from first to third positions. It was a method of motivation that encouraged us to work hard to get the best possible positions in our class every year.

Additionally, we had a hefty reputation to live up to in our village. Education was highly valued in our hamlet. Our parents esteemed our educational prowess to such a degree that we worked very hard so they would be pleased with us. My family really treasured education, knowing that it was the key to our future success. We carried our shoulders high to make our parents proud. To crown it all, my eldest sister, the late Mrs. Dorah Konkwo Ovuike (Nee Ebiringa), won the Etiti Local Government Area Scholarship that placed her in the renowned Elelenwa Girls' Secondary School in Port Harcourt in the early 1960s. Her academic brilliance granted her the opportunity to proceed to the University Teaching Hospital (UNTH) in Ibadan, Nigeria. On her graduation, she became the first Registered Nurse (RN) in Etiti Local Govermenment Area (comprising Obowo, Ihitte, and Uboma)—all in Imo state. Our family was very proud of her.

As a village boy, I learned how to cook at the early age of ten, even though cooking in the kitchen at that time in our Igbo culture was regarded as women's work.

Little Umutukuru, Umuariam, Imo State in Nigeria con-tributed a lot in making me the man I am today. Later in my life when I served in the Nigerian Youth Service, I was able to cook for my fellow "Corpers," Christian and otherwise, pro-viding delicious meals for them. Some were almost jealous of me because they never had the opportunity to learn to cook. In truth, I am proud to have been a village boy. It developed in me much more than a strong work ethic. It also gave me other skills. As a village boy, I was involved in providing grass for our livestock as well as cooking.

These positions of service called for humility and compas-sion. You cannot close your ears when your family's animals (and those of your whole village) are hungry and crying for food. They are depending on you and you alone, so you quickly find them what they need. I learned to be very focused on serv-ing them and caring for them. The well-being of our entire vil-lage depended on them, so even though it seemed like a lowly kind of job, it really wasn't. It was actually an important job. So many in things in life turn out like that!

It is through these seemingly smaller tasks that we learn how to handle bigger things and develop perseverance so we can stay committed to the work God gives us. Jesus spoke about this idea in the parable of the talents. To the man who used his talents well, Jesus said, "His lord said unto him, Well done, good and faithful servant; thou hast been faithful over a few things, I will make thee ruler over many things: enter thou into the joy of thy lord" (Matt. 25:23).

Chapter Three

The Value of Commitment

Being a village boy exposed me to the value of commitment. Frankly speaking, your environment may hide you from opportunities or expose you to opportunities. I have heard the testimonies of Christians who have left megachurches to go to small churches because the smaller group afforded them the opportunity to serve and enhance their talents or gifts in a way the mega-group could not. The state of your dedication to a course defines your level of success. David was committed to the caring of their sheep in the bush, no matter the cost. He was disciplined and selfless; subsequently, he was a successful shepherd boy.

I remembered the first time I was given an assignment in our local church. Two other boys and myself were appointed by our assembly pastor to be chorus leaders during church worship. That was the first time in my life to mount the podium before the congregation to lead the chorus. Just a teenager, I was gripped with nervousness. Sweat dripped off my body like drops of rain. But because I was committed to it, I did well and I never experienced this level of nerves again when I did this. Today when I reflect on it, I thank the Almighty God who gave me the courage and strength to be committed to it. Three teenagers were appointed for the assignment. One guy made silly excuses whenever his turn to lead came. Sadly, he never made it in life. I do challenge the youth of today:

> *Let no one despise your youth.*
> (1 Timothy 4:12a NKJV)

> *And whatever your hand finds to do, do it with your might.*
> (Ecclesiastes 9:10 NKJV)

That reminds me of when Jesus found Philip, a man from Bethsaida, and he became His disciple. Philip found Nathaniel and said, "We have found Him of whom Moses in the law and also the prophets wrote—Jesus of Nazareth, the son of Joseph" (John 1:45 NKJV). Do you know what Nathaniel replied? He said, "Can anything good come out of Nazareth?" And who were they talking about? Jesus Himself!

The fact that you are born a village boy does not diminish your destiny. Jesus the Warrior, King of all kings, was born in a little town called Bethlehem. Your place of birth at times promotes your identity, but the fact that you were born in the poorest family in that village should not be a stigma. Your place of birth does not decide your reputation. Before you were born, God knew you: "Before I formed you in the womb I knew you; Before you were born I sanctified you; I ordained you a prophet to the nations" (Jer. 1:5 NKJV). This was the word of God to the young prophet Jeremiah, so God can use your place of birth to advertise you. God can use your family of birth to identify you and make you royalty.

David, the youngest son of Jesse, was born a village shepherd boy in Bethlehem, a small town in the hill country of Judah. Bethlehem was later called "the city of David" (Luke 2:4, 11). David was not only a village boy, but also a shepherd boy, meaning he was on the bottom rung, the lowest level of the village boys in prestige. But guess what? He was very committed as a shepherd boy. He cared for the sheep to such an extent that he risked his life for them. One day a lion came to eat the sheep in his custody. He killed that lion. He chose to chance his own death rather than see his sheep die and then have to tell his father that a lion had devoured their sheep. On another day, a bear came to try his luck. David chased the bear and killed it. The lion and the bear became food for the family.

What a hero! A lowly shepherd boy had killed a lion and a bear. They did no harm to him, not a scratch. David knew that he was in for training. Commitment promotes our destiny. It is a ladder that helps us reach the peak of the mountaintop. David was not only committed to the caring of the sheep, but also to his loyalty to God, the Supreme Commander and Master of the Universe. What on earth tells you that David killed the lion and the bear by himself? How many people have you heard that killed a lion other than David? In the Old Testament, the prophet Samuel tells King Saul:

> But now your kingdom shall not continue. The Lord has sought for Himself a man after His own heart, and the Lord has commanded him to be commander over His people, because you have not kept what the Lord commanded you.
>
> (1 Samuel 13:14 NKJV)

Much, much later in the New Testament, when Paul is preaching he speaks of David and his unique place in their history:

> And afterward they asked for a king; so God gave them Saul the son of Kish, a man of the tribe of Benjamin, for forty years. And when He had removed him, He raised up for them David as king, to whom also He gave testimony and said, "I have found David the son of Jesse, a man

> *after My own heart, who will do all My will." From this*
> *man's seed, according to the promise, God raised up for*
> *Israel a Savior—Jesus.*
>
> (Acts 13:21–23 NKJV)

A man after God's own heart! And from David's house came our Lord and Savior, Jesus. David, the second king of Israel was so consumed in his relationship with the God of heaven that he discovered the food that God loves so much—praise. God inhabits the praises of his people.[6] David played a stringed instrument skillfully and wrote poems while he was taking care of the sheep.

---

6   See Psalm 22:3.

Chapter Four

School Days

In 1966, my brother graduated from the University of Nigeria Nsukka. He immediately got a job with the Eastern Nigeria Development Cooperation in Calabar in Cross River State, first with Kwa Falls Estate and then Calaro Oil Palm Estate of that same company. The day he told me to get ready to come and live with him in Calabar, I was the happiest person in the village. I would be leaving my village for the first time in my entire life, and on top of that, relocating to an urban area. As a matter of fact, I started gathering and storing firewood for my mother so that my absence would not create any problems for her. I didn't want anything to make my brother change his mind about allowing me to leave the village and live with him. Surprisingly, month after month the plan was postponed, until it was put off indefinitely.

In the following year of 1967, I gained admission into Ife Grammar School in Mbaise. I was very happy, not only because I had graduated into high school, but even more because I had to relocate and live in a new environment altogether. Living in a hostel with fellow students and enjoying such amenities like electricity for the first time made my new life much different and exciting. In this community, there were challenges too. In fact, it is life's challenges that groom us and lead us into perfection and stability.

There was no time to waste in boarding school. From five o'clock in the morning to ten o'clock at night, a student's community life is full of challenges. The class one students, popularly called freshers, our slang term for tadpoles, were subjected to rigorous tasks and activities without much breathing space. The student had no right to challenge this discipline. From the moment a student woke from sleep in the morning, the fresher began with morning chores. Subsequently, that same student would rush to the stream owned and managed by Mr. Nwanjoku to fetch water for the kitchen for the cooking of the students' food. Surprisingly, this water for the kitchen became the students' meal ticket. This same class one student will fetch water for the senior student he served and knew as his neighbor. That neighbor might be a final year (five) or form four student, as the case may be. At times the new student may end up serving both the form five and the form four student. Nevertheless, the other senior students (class two) made life somehow miserable for the freshers. Instead of doing their own jobs, they depended on the new group of students for their water supply. Any time any class one student showed resistance, the class two students ganged up on him and punished him, forcing him to kneel down or be beaten up.

As mentioned before, the water the students fetched for the kitchen became their meal ticket for the day. If a student failed to fetch water, he had to share his meal that day, which meant he didn't get much to eat. Our lifestyle developed tough skin. Those students who came from urban areas were the worst-affected of the lot of us. Those who came from rural areas were better prepared. All the same, we had no regrets because we knew we were there for a purpose.

Our goal to be educated well became our driving force. Some students forfeited their meals and depended on bread and tea for days. At the end of the day, our focus on our studies overwhelmingly overshadowed all ill-treatment. We enjoyed the dedicated teachers we had. They taught us with enthusiasm and a readiness to impart their knowledge. While the morning schedule was for academics, the evening session was full of extracurricular activities like sports and games. I loved running cross-country, a mile-long race around the Ife community. Each day's activity ended with a special evening preparation between 7:00 p.m. and 9:00 p.m. At the end of our prep time came the evening devotion, where hymns, songs, and prayers rolled down like water. No matter how jammed the day's activity were, 10:00 p.m. was junior lights out time, marking the end of the day for all the students except the class fives. By this law, any junior student who was not in his bed by that time was in big trouble.

I enjoyed Sunday worship service in the school auditorium. These meetings were the culmination of the week and a time of real celebration. The school organist, Mr. Charles Nwanguma, played while we sang from hymn books: either *Songs of Praise* or *Ancient and Modern with Cathedral Psalter*. One of my favorites was "Abide with Me," which we sang during the evening prayer at the end of each prep schedule. The students always sang the line, "In life, in death, oh, Lord, abide with me," with gusto. Despite the maltreatment and torture we endured at the hands of the year two students because we were freshers, we loved school. We still had long tails like tadpoles and we knew those tails would not be cut off for an entire year, but we were still glad to be there. The college boy life here overwhelmed the village boy mentality, but I did get to visit home.

I still remembered weekend off days when we visited home in our white-on-whites (white shirt and white shorts), dressed in white canvas sneakers. Whenever I got home, I was filled with pride and dignity. I was in paradise compared to my other mates who were still in the village, and living without unprecedented privilege. I loved my old school days. The training and discipline we received molded my character and intrigued my mind. I learned how to think tremendously. One of the things I remember well was: "Eating with sets." The first thing students learned in the dining hall was to eat with a knife and fork, with the fork in your left hand and knife in your right. Several times, the senior students would check to find those who were violating this rule. Whenever they caught a victim, the price was their food. Their meal was instantly gone—immediately shared with those sitting at their table. Each long table accommodated about eight students in a double row, facing each other. The unfortunate soul who didn't use his knife and fork properly and got caught had no choice but to leave the dining hall with an empty stomach.

I also enjoyed the prep time after dinner. No student had the option not to be in the prep room studying. In this way, the students spent time wisely—either by doing assignments, reading relevant books, or solving math problems. There was always roll call prior to our prep time and was repeated at the end. If any student was caught daydreaming or loitering during the prep time, he would be cutting grass during his lunch the following day or fetching water for the kitchen. In our community, every minute counted. Any student who passed through the walls of our school emerged disciplined. Otherwise, he would never be useful to himself or society. Sadly, our noble school life was cut short by civil war.

I will never forget the summons of an emergency gathering of all the students in May of 1967 in the school auditorium. The headline in all the papers that day was: "The Zero Hour Has Come." That slogan became a reality on the night of May 30, 1967. According to the announcement made by the school principal, Mr. Anyiam, Lt. Colonel Ojukwu (the Biafran general), declared us as part of the Sovereign State of Biafra in a speech that began our fight for independence from Nigeria. As a result, the school was closed indefinitely because war between Nigeria and Biafra was imminent.

Chapter Five

The Ravages of War

No condition is permanent in this world.

(an Ibo saying)

(Editor's Note: This chapter is dependent on outside sources to verify exact information, so please have grace for the necessary inclusions. Sources are cited in footnotes, so you can easily access the facts, and read about it more on your own.)

To understand our civil war, you need to understand a few facts about Nigeria that you might not know. Nigeria is one of the most populous countries in the world and sits on a giant reservoir of oil. If Biafra had seceded from Nigeria without all that oil, we may have been successful in forming our own government, and continuing as our own nation to this day.[7] But that is not what happened.

As I already mentioned, the Ibo are known as a hard-working people, which is a great blessing, but success makes enemies too. In our case, while some in our country looked at the Ibo people as thrifty and industrious, devoted to making their way, and very focused on bettering themselves through a good education that could lead to higher-paying jobs, others

---

7   Frederick Forsyth, *The Biafra Story* (Middlesex, England: Penguin Books Ltd., 1969).

chose to regard us with suspicion, envy, and hate, not unlike the way the Nazis looked at the Jews in 1933.[8] Nigeria is home to many tribes and more languages, so we have always been an extremely diverse nation. Additionally, we had longstanding British ties to our oil, much of which was in Biafran territory, and we had a recipe for disaster. Understanding all this underlying tension is important to understanding what follows.

I vividly remember October 1, 1960. It was my second year in primary school, and with jubilation, I joined with my classmates as we celebrated Nigeria's first Independence Day. Nigeria had been under British colonial rule since the mid-1800s, which was an amazing moment for our country. Students were given free cups adorned with the green-and-white Nigerian flag and free food too. Everyone was happy that Nigeria was no longer run by the British government. Dr. Azikiwe was the president while Sir Abubakar Tafawa Balewa was the prime minister. I was only seven years old, and everything seemed okay, even peaceful. Agriculture was booming, evidenced by how well my father and my uncle were trading in oil palm produce, which was exported to Britain. My father and my uncle were both successful businessmen in our community.

The southern section of Nigeria exported cocoa to make chocolate, while the northern part was second to none in exporting groundnuts. The Eastern Region (my own region) supplied the world with palm produce. Eventually, war would deprive us of our peace and bring our economy crashing down to nothing. What follows is a brief history of this war.

In 1966, the people of Nigeria witnessed the most traumatic and bloody coup d'état in our history. It was the genesis of the tragic Nigeria-Biafra Civil War which would follow in

---

8   Ibid.

1967. The coup began on January 15, 1966, when "mutinous Nigeria soldiers led by Major Chukwuma Nzeogwu and Major Emmanuel Ifeajuna killed twenty-two people including the prime minister, many senior politicians, many senior Army officers (and their wives), as well as the sentinels on protective duty at the time."[9]

Major General Johnson Aguiyi-Ironsi became the new head of state (and its first military one); Hassan Katsina became the military governor of Northern Nigeria; and Odumegwu Ojukwu became the military governor for the Eastern Region. Unfortunately, at roughly midnight on July 28, 1966, a counter-coup was masterminded by Lt. Colonel Muhammed "as a reaction to the recent killings of Northern politicians and officers by some soldiers"[10] during the first coup in January. Aguiyi-Ironsi and others were killed, and Yakubu Gowon became the head of state on August 1, 1966, until July 29, 1975.[11]

Next came anti-Igbo pogroms.[12] These were "a series of massacres committed against Igbo people and other people of southern Nigerian origin living in Northern Nigeria starting in May 1966 and reaching a peak after September 1966. Between 8,000 and 30,000 Igbos and easterners have been estimated to have been killed."[13] This traumatized the whole nation and

9   "1966 Nigerian Coup D'état." Wikipedia. Wikimedia Foundation, January 17, 2023. Accessed February 3, 2023. https://en.wikipedia.org/wiki/1966_Nigerian_coup.
10   "1966 Nigerian Counter-Coup," Wikipedia (Wikimedia Foundation, September 11, 2022), https://en.wikipedia.org/wiki/1966_Nigerian_counter-coup.
11   Ibid.
12   The terms Igbo and Ibo are interchangeable. This people group is one of the largest in Africa, and can be found in many countries besides Nigeria.
13   "1966 Anti-Igbo Pogrom," Wikipedia (Wikimedia Foundation, Janu-

filled the land with turmoil. Fear and paranoia ravaged the entire people.

After the deaths of so many Ibo in the North, they no longer felt secure there and fled. With the goal of living in Nigeria in peace, Igbo leaders and Governor Ojukwu began a series of peace talks to see a way out of the looming threat of war. The Aburi Accord was reached at a unique meeting that was "attended by delegates of both the Federal Government of Nigeria (the supreme Military Council) and the Eastern Region led by Colonel ... Ojukwu." [14] However, the British government warned President Gowon in the North *not* to implement the Aburi Accord. Instead of working on the new agreement, Gowon drafted a decree that made a mockery of its resolutions.

Ojukwu was not satisfied and further insisted on a reorganization of the army on a regional basis. Gowon was firmly opposed to splitting up the army. This political debate triggered the popular slogan: "On Aburi, we stand" (by Ojukwu). Thus, the refusal of the Nigerian military government to follow the Aburi Accord led to the declaration of Biafra as a nation. In answer, Gowon declared war against Biafra. The conflict devastated Biafra for three years.

On July 6, 1967, the Nigeria launched a full-scale invasion into Biafra. In that first year, the first invasion was of Onitsha from October 4 to October 12, 1967, taking city after city during that year. As a result, millions of refugees flooded Biafra land.

"Within a year, Nigerian government troops surrounded Biafra, and captured coastal oil facilities and the city of Port

---

ary 11, 2023), https://en.wikipedia.org/wiki/1966_anti-Igbo_pogrom.
14   "Aburi Accord," Wikipedia (Wikimedia Foundation, August 21, 2022), https://en.wikipedia.org/wiki/Aburi_Accord.

Harcourt. A blockade was imposed as a deliberate policy during the ensuing stalemate which led to the mass starvation of Biafran civilians. During the two-and-half years of the war, there were about 100,000 overall military casualties, while between 500,000 and 2 million Biafran civilians died of starvation."[15] Schools were completely closed. Hunger and *kwarshiokor*, a very severe form of malnutrition, killed many children and pregnant women because of a lack of protein.

On the other hand, the result of being blockaded transformed the mindset of the Biafrans. They manufactured their own weapons (landmines, armored tanks, bombs, and grenades). However, Biafra needed more than that to win against a better armed and more powerful army. With their civilian population starving, they appealed to the world for help.

"The Biafran government reported that Nigeria was using hunger and genocide to win the war, and sought aid from the outside world. Private groups in the US, led by Senator Ted Kennedy, responded. No one was ever held responsible for these killings."[16] Though some countries such as Gabon and Ivory Coast and others recognized Biafra, they were not strong enough to effectively help.

As mentioned earlier, Britain's primary concern was Nigeria's oil, so they supported the Northern government and resisted Biafra. Many countries remained officially neutral, including the United States. This meant that most relief came through different charitable organizations, such as the Red Cross and Caritas Internationalis, a worldwide Catholic relief organization. Some aid was flown in, but much of it was

---

15   "Nigerian Civil War," Wikipedia (Wikimedia Foundation, January 30, 2023), https://en.wikipedia.org/wiki/Nigerian_Civil_War.
16   Ibid.

blocked. As a result, the Biafran people suffered the trauma of starvation, in addition to continual air raids and other atrocities.

"The war cost the Igbos a great deal.... More than half a million people died from the famine imposed deliberately through blockade.... Lack of medicine also contributed. Thousands ... starved to death every day as the war progressed.... The Red Cross in September 1968 estimated 8,000–10,000 deaths from starvation each day. The leader of a Nigerian peace conference delegation said in 1968 that 'starvation is a legitimate weapon of war and we have every intention of using it against the rebels.' This stance is generally considered to reflect the policy of the Nigerian government"[17] at the time. After enduring thirty months of warfare, Biafra surrendered in 1970.

In the end, an estimated three million people died, most of them Biafrans. A great number of people died from starvation and diseases associated with the war, while many others lost their lives from the relentless bombings and mass executions enacted upon the civilian population. It is unimaginable and unthinkable that to this day, no one has been held to account for the untold war crime atrocities that were committed against humanity in that war. The Biafran war was not unlike others around the world, both in times past and in the present day; war atrocities that have compelled the international community to cry out for justice and accountability. In those other situations, the culprits had been summoned to face their war crimes, but in the Biafran case, even after more than fifty years since the end of that war, the world is still waiting for justice on behalf of the innocent civilian population that was targeted and killed.

---

17   Ibid.

Where was the village boy during the Nigeria – Biafra War (1967 to 1970)?

As I stated in my previous narrative, the day I left the four corners of Ife Grammar School, Mbaise, Imo state, Nigeria, back to the village because of the breakout of the war, life dramatically and drastically changed. Day after day my thinking faculty was filled with, "When will the war end? When will I go back to school which has in no little way affected my whole mindset?" All my wishes became a mirage for three full years. Each day appeared as it was today or tomorrow. Day after day the story remained the same. Back to the village now became real.

As a teenager, I was not conscripted into the army as many young adults were forcefully initiated into the military. Some became Navy officers, some Air Force cadets, some Army officers. For the fact that both primary and tertiary institutions in Biafra were closed, the only alternative for these vibrant young adults was to join the military. However, I joined my parents in their farm work. On the other hand, I engaged myself in fishing and trapping of rats and rabbits. As a result of the blockage for the entire Eastern Nigeria at that time, there was no importation of real nutritional food for the common people. The only source of protein was farfetched except from rats and rabbits and other bush meat we caught each day we went out for hunting.

We lived in the outskate, interior central Igbo land. In the hit of the war, every school in our community become a refugee camp. Despite that, the trauma of daily air raid of the Nigeria fighters and bombers ravaged both the nearby metropolitan areas and the suburban areas. These planes hovered over our rural areas in their attempt to bomb the nearby metropolitan areas where civilians live. Every day we carried our hearts in our hands as we tried to hide from one place to the other against the air raid. The grace of God was on us that we never vacated as refugees. As a matter of fact, the majority of the villagers became regular worshipers of God, each day making one resolution or the other seeking God's protection from the horror of war. All the churches in the rural areas became cities of refuge for both indigenes and non-indigenes for shelter from the war. No one knew when it was going to end. To the glory of God I was among those who received special grace; because of my age I was never conscripted into the military nor molested in any way. I was an eyewitness to our vibrant, brilliant young men who were killed during one air raid or the other as they were brought home from urban areas. I will never forget a day that six coffins loaded in a big truck arrived in my village. The bearers delivered one of them in our village, a young scientist who was killed during an explosion blast in their ammunition manufacturing laboratory. I witnessed another handsome young man who was killed during an air raid in a nearby urban city brought home for burial.

My eldest brother, Elder/Engineer Victor C. B. Ebiringa, was one of the engineers with the Research and Production (RAP) Department for the manufacturing of landmines, rockets, and ammunitions. God protected him and every other member of Ebiringa's family. The promises of God are "yes and amen"—very real. The Book of Numbers, chapter 31, verse 49, says, "And they said to Moses, 'Your servants have taken a count of the men of war who are under our command, and not a man of us is missing.'" Psalms chapter 118, verse 17, says, "I shall not die, but live, and declare the works of the LORD" (NKJV). Obviously, it is incumbent on me to give this TESTIMONY so that people will glorify the name of God. I have to conclude with this song, "WHEN I think of the goodness of Jesus, and what He has done for me, my very soul shall shout Hallelujah! Praise God for saving me."

Chapter Six

Picking Up the Pieces

When the war ended, life was very tough, very challenging. In Biafra, Biafran money was replaced by the Nigerian pound and shilling. People took up all kinds of menial jobs and trading to get pounds and shillings. I carried a four-gallon tin of oil on my head all the way from my village of Umuariam to Umuahia (a distance of twelve miles) to sell it in order to get pounds and shillings so we could make ends meet. We would set off as early as 8:00 p.m. and arrive at our destination at 6:00 a.m. on the morning of the following day. After selling the oil we had money for food. During this difficult time period, people rarely ate one square meal a day.

On a good note, our schools, which had been closed for a period of three years, now reopened. There was mass promotion. Those who were in class one before the war were promoted to class two, while those who were in primary six became the class one students in the secondary schools. Students were allowed to either go to their original schools before the war or choose a new school of their choice.

I went back to Ife Grammar School where I had been in 1967. Two years later, I transferred to Union Secondary School. At last, I was able to finally live with my brother who was still an employee of the Eastern Nigeria Development Corporation.

From his home, I could walk to school every day. However, my younger brother, Daniel, who had been my companion at Ife Grammar School, stayed there, where he took his West African School Certificate Examination.

Very slowly, life returned to some semblance of normal.

Chapter Seven

My Turning Point

I had been born into a religious family, and my father was a good disciplinarian. Nevertheless, in my childhood until about the age of twelve or so, a spirit of rebellion reigned in me. I was disrespectful, angry, and stubborn. I fought against those in authority over me as well as with others my age. I stole and was not submitted in my heart to God.

It wasn't until I entered secondary school around the age of fourteen that I began to have a sense of yearning for God. I could taste a seeking for God inside of me, but alas! When I would do good, evil was present with me. During that adolescent period, I became religiously inclined so as to be almost a Christian. My moral standard became conspicuously high in the community. Most probably would have considered me a Christian, but unknown to those around me, there was a huge struggle raging inside of me. To crown it all, I had no peace.

I read the Bible and prayed occasionally, but these were mere formalities. In the actual sense they had no meaning to me. Even though I sang melodiously as a chorister, I could sense no real life in it. I felt like I had no alternative except to warm up seats on Sundays and stay active the best I could. I felt trapped in religion. A strong yearning to know the way out built in me until I began to feel more and more desperate.

Unfortunately, even though I was in church, no one gave me the adequate antidote I needed—to show me the way.

The straw that broke the camel's back struck when I changed school in 1972 to Boys' High School Awkunanaw Enugu. On that eventful Sunday afternoon, a Christian fellowship meeting was organized by the Scripture Union. The preacher, Brother Onwuchekwa, spoke vehemently on "Where Will You Spend Eternity?" He emphasized the need for one to receive Christ at the acceptable time (that is, during one's lifetime).[18] He stressed that one could only spend eternity in heaven on the basis of confessing, forsaking one's sins, and inviting Jesus into one's heart. He said only Christ could give us power to live above sin and be a Christian.[19] Christ is the only way, the truth, and the life.[20] Only through Him could we reach the Father. He said Christ died to pardon us and cleanse us from the sin of the whole world. Immediately, I saw the need to confess my sins and accept Jesus into my heart, so I did. On that day, Jesus became my personal Savior.

Immediately after my conversion, old things passed away and all things became new according to 2 Corinthians 5:17. Two remarkable things happened as a result of the grace of God upon my life. First, I had peace in my mind. I took ownership of Ephesians 2:14 as my life verse: "For he is our peace, who hath made both one, and had broken down the middle wall of partition between us."

The other big change was obvious: My tongue was redeemed! No longer did I speak twisted words. No more twaddle, no more idle, and no more abusive words for me. They

---

18   See 2 Corinthians 6:2.
19   See John 1:12.
20   See John 14:6.

were replaced with praise. I began to bless the name of God every day with psalms and spiritual songs. Witnessing for Christ became my spiritual exercise. My new birth gave me a deep zeal to know God more. My desire increased as I began to read and study my Bible daily with understanding according to 2 Timothy 2:15. Enjoying fellowship with fellow believers continued to stimulate my spiritual appetite and became a great pleasure. Now I pressed toward "the mark for the prize of the high calling of God in Christ Jesus" (Phil. 3:14).

Chapter Eight

The Reality of the Holy Spirit

I was immediately challenged as I began to learn about God and Jesus and the Holy Spirit. My beliefs about the Holy Spirit were new ground. Many biblical passages fascinated me and eventually changed my mindset from what they had been before.

One was Jesus's words when He said,

But you shall receive power when the Holy Ghost has come upon you: and you shall be witnesses to Me in Jerusalem, and in all Judea and Samaria, and to the end of the earth.
(Acts 1:8 NKJV)

This passage instilled in me the potency of the dynamite deposit Jesus made in every believer. There should be no stagnation in a Christian. The power of the Holy Ghost is a driving force that gives a Christian the ability to witness for Christ and live in the power of God on a daily basis. I had been a timid village boy, but when this hidden power exploded in me, my shyness disappeared. Another section of the Bible was what Paul wrote:

And it came to pass, that, while Apollos was at Corinth, Paul having passed through the upper coasts came to Ephesus: and

> *finding certain disciples, he said unto them, Have ye received*
> *the Holy Ghost since ye believed?... And when Paul had laid his*
> *hands upon them, the Holy Ghost came on them; and they spa-*
> *ke with tongues, and prophesied.*
>
> (Acts 19:1–2, 6)

I believe in the power of the Holy Ghost *verbatim*—just as it is
written. I believe in the speaking of tongues. I believe in prophecy. All these are the result and signs that follow whoever believes in Jesus.

> *And these signs shall follow them that believe; in my name shall*
> *they cast out devils; they shall speak with new tongues; they*
> *shall take up serpents; and if they drink any deadly thing, it*
> *shall not hurt them; they shall lay hands on the sick, and they*
> *shall recover.*
>
> (Mark 16:17–18)

The pursuit of the Holy Spirit leads to an increased hunger for
righteousness, as it says in the Sermon on the Mount: "Blessed
are those who hunger and thirst for righteousness, for they
shall be filled" (Matt. 5:6). I do not know about you, but for me,
the hunger to live in right standing with God, living a righteous
life, and the pursuit after the baptism of the Holy Spirit nearly
drove me crazy. If you are a Christian, do not be so complacent
and stay in your comfort zone over the matter of the filling of
the Holy Spirit. As a Christian, our body now is the temple of
the Holy Spirit. He requires sanctity, and a continual filling, so
that we are always reserved for the Master's use. This temple
must receive the Holy Spirit.

> *Know ye not that ye are the temple of God, and that the Spirit*
> *of God dwelleth in you?*
>
> (1 Corinthians 3:16)

And when he had said this, he breathed on them, and saith unto them, Receive ye the Holy Ghost.

(John 20:22)

And be not drunk with wine, wherein is excess; but be filled with the Spirit

(Ephesians 5:18)

Until one is filled with wine, the spirit of intoxication (called Abaddon in the Bible) does not possess him. In the same way, until a believer is completely filled with the Holy Spirit, the person will not be intoxicated by the Holy Ghost. This is important because it is the Holy Spirit that gives us direction. He's our divine GPS! It's no wonder that Paul writes, "For as many as are led by the Spirit of God, they are the sons of God" [or Spirit-filled] (Rom. 8:14).

The moment I became born again I began to earnestly desire to receive the Holy Spirit's baptism. I observed my quiet time with God every morning and every night. I read my Bible from Genesis to Revelation several times. I attended crusades and Christian fellowships. I waited on the Lord with prayer and fasting. I will not forget that special night in December 1972 when something unusual and spectacular happened to me. I was at a village church prayer meeting attended by mostly women; I and the pastor were the only men in attendance. As Pastor Isaiah Elewechi Job Onwuasoanya was praying, the power of God descended on me with uncontrollable emotion. Instantly, I began to speak in an unknown tongue. I never knew when my tongue moved from speaking my native dialect to an unknown language. I was overwhelmed, and could not control myself. My voice was so loud that my family members in our house next to the church were wondering what was *wrong* with me when I returned home at the end of the meeting. Well, I narrated the story of the beginning of my Holy Ghost journey. Glory to God!

Chapter Nine

The Gifts of the Holy Spirit

A man's gift maketh room for him, and bringeth him before great men.

(Proverbs 18:16)

Immediately after I received the baptism of the Holy Spirit, I had a new and unique experience. I started speaking in tongues. Whenever I opened my mouth to pray either in Igbo or English, I began to speak in an unknown tongue which I didn't understand. When I inquired, my pastor told me it could be heavenly, even an angelic language, or another language, such as German or Spanish. After a while, I was taught how to control it, but it took some time. On the day I received Jesus as my personal Savior, I remembered how the Holy Ghost had transformed my tongue, making room for something supernatural. Once I began speaking in tongues, I controlled it in the congregation of the believers, but in my private devotions, I delighted in it and desired to pray in tongues as long as the Holy Spirit could lead me under His unction.

The baptism of the Holy Spirit is the beginning of a spiritual journey with the third person of the Trinity (the Holy Ghost). Jesus made these promises in John:

> *And I will pray the Father, and he shall give you another*
> *Comforter, that he may abide with you for ever; even the Spirit*
> *of truth.*
>
> (John 14:16–17a)

> *Howbeit when he, the Spirit of truth, is come, he will guide you*
> *into all truth: for he shall not speak of himself; but whatsoever*
> *he shall hear, that shall he speak: and he will shew you things to*
> *come.*
>
> (John 16:13)

The Holy Spirit is a person that empowers you as your spiritual partner. He directs you; He comforts you; and He builds your faith to do the extraordinary by giving you a supernatural mindset from above. The apostle Jude confirms this by writing this encouragement: "But ye, beloved, building up yourselves on your most holy faith, praying in the Holy Ghost" (Jude 1:20).

The Holy Spirit—through the power of the tongue—helps me to pray even when I am short of words. When I pray in tongues for a long time, the Spirit gives me some inspiration that helps me solve problems and even brings healing to both my spiritual and physical being. The apostle Paul attested to this fact in Romans 8:26 when he wrote, "Likewise the Spirit also helpeth our infirmities: for we know not what we should pray for as we ought: but the Spirit itself maketh intercession for us with groanings which cannot be uttered." Holy Ghost power enables me to pray, read, and study the Bible *pari passu* (on "equal footing" with Him).

The journey of speaking in tongues will take you to another level and bring you to knowing your spiritual gifts. Often your area of calling is determined by the gifts that God gives to you. Frankly speaking, my spiritual gifts transformed my mindset (my whole being). One day I was reading 1 Corinthians 14, and a particular section fascinated me and captured my attention.

> *Follow after charity, and desire spiritual gifts, but rather that ye may prophesy. For he that speaketh in an unknown tongue speaketh not unto men, but unto God: for no man understandeth him; howbeit in the spirit he speaketh mysteries. But he that prophesieth speaketh unto men to edification, and exhortation, and comfort. He that speaketh in an unknown tongue edifieth himself, but he that prophesieth edifieth the church.*
> (1 Corinthians 14:1–4)

From that day onward, I started praying for the gift of prophecy. Although other sections of the Bible mention more gifts, 1 Corinthians 12 outlines nine specific ones:

> *Now concerning spiritual gifts, brethren, I would not have you ignorant.... Now there are diversities of gifts, but the same Spirit.... But the manifestation of the Spirit is given to every man to profit withal. For to one is given by the Spirit the word of wisdom; to another the word of knowledge by the same Spirit. To another faith by the same Spirit; to another the gifts of healing by the same Spirit; to another the working of miracles; to another prophecy; to another discerning of spirits; to another divers kinds of tongues; to another the interpretation of tongues.*
> (1 Corinthians 12:1, 4, 7–10)

In summary, these nine gifts of the Holy Spirit are the word of wisdom, the word of knowledge, the gift of faith, gifts of healing, the working of miracles, prophecy, discerning of spirits, divers kinds of tongues, and the interpretation of tongues.

Chapter Ten

Waiting on the Word of God

I did not receive the gift of prophecy immediately when I asked for it, but that fact did not make me question the authenticity of the Word of God. Instead, the waiting rooted me in my faith more firmly. In one instance during that time, I started thinking that the devil was trying to rob me of God's promise to me. At that time (and in countless ones since) I backed up my faith with the Word of God, and quenched his flaming darts by wielding the sword of the Spirit with the Word of truth as it says in Ephesians 6. In this particular case, it was these verses that helped me:

> And from the days of John the Baptist until now the kingdom of heaven suffereth violence, and the violent take it by force.
> (Matthew 11:12)

> But we will give ourselves continually to prayer, and to the ministry of the word.
> (Acts 6:4)

After reading this, I implemented the strategy described above. Fasting became a daily affair. Through prayer and fasting, God's hidden *dunamis* (strength and power) inside me just exploded. I became a source of blessing to many, just as God told Abraham that he would be: "I will bless thee, and make thy name great;

and thou shalt be a blessing" (Gen. 12:2b). Whatever gifts God has blessed you with—spiritual or material—are meant to be used to bless others. The more you bless others, the more your life and resources will flow like a river of living water, a pure and life-giving spring of water. Speaking of us, the Bible says:

> *He shall be like a tree planted by the rivers of water, that brings forth his fruit in its season; whose leaf also shall not wither; and whatever he does shall prosper.*
>
> (Psalm 1:3 NKJV)

> *But whosoever drinketh of the water that I shall give him shall never thirst; but the water that I shall give him shall be in him a well of water springing up into everlasting life.*
>
> (John 4:14)

Chapter Eleven

Beyond My Imagination: The Gift of Prophecy

Ask, and it shall be given you; seek and ye shall find; knock and it shall be opened unto you.

(Matthew 7:7)

If ye then, being evil, know how to give good gifts unto your children: how much more shall your heavenly Father give the Holy Spirit to them that ask him?

(Luke 11:13)

The Bible is the true Word of God, authentic and accurate in every way. If you believe what the Bible promises, you will see the manifestation of that promise. When Jesus said we should "ask and it shall be given you [us]," He meant we would receive that which we asked for based on His Word. In the next verse, Jesus was comforting His followers about how much the Father wanted to give His Holy Spirit to those who came to Him. He continues to pour Himself out for His children today, just as He did then. The truth is that whatever you ask for, you receive, including the Holy Spirit and the gift of the Holy Spirit. I asked a sister if she spoke in tongues, and she said no. However, she is a believer and has been a church usher for many years! Beloved, the gift of the Holy Spirit is readily available for you upon request. On the day of Pentecost, Peter spoke vehemently and boldly:

> *And ye shall receive the gift of the Holy Ghost. For the promise is unto you, and to your children, and to all that are afar off, even as many as the Lord our God shall call.*
>
> (Acts 2:38b–39)

Just as Jesus died for the whole world (as in *everyone*), so the gift of the Holy Ghost (His promise) is for both Jews and Gentiles alike—literally for everyone who believes.

In 1975, the Holy Ghost manifested the gift of prophecy in me beyond my imagination. In the presence of my father, the late Ugwuobodo Isaac Ebiringa and my younger brother, Dr. Daniel Ebiringa (now an elder), I prophesied that God would take me to the United States. I didn't know when or how it would happen, but the same message continued to ring in my ears. I knew it was the word of the Lord over my life. As a result, I watched for every opportunity that opened before me. In my heart, I wondered how it would happen. *Possibly it will be this way or that way,* I pondered, but no matter what, I knew and had faith that it was going to happen somehow.

In 1978, I was offered in-service training to study at Pennsylvania State University in State College, Pennsylvania. When all the preparations had been concluded, the Imo state school education board personnel manager and director who was to sign the bond paper, shocked me by refusing to sign the agreement that would have covered both the school fees and my flight. I was very upset, and I wept bitterly; in the end, I had to trust God to open another door, which He did.

I received the Nigeria Federal Government Scholarship that enabled me to study in Nigeria, and I graduated as a mathematics teacher. I taught for seventeen years in various secondary schools in Imo state in Nigeria, and also got married and had six children: three daughters and three sons! I am grateful to the Almighty who empowered me to affect the lives of many students as well as others academically, socially, and spiritually during this time. I came to trust the word of the Lord more and more deeply. Whatever good plan God has for you, it is His prerogative to determine how and when He will do it. Just trust and obey. Listen to this passage:

> For my thoughts are not your thoughts, neither are your ways my ways, saith the LORD. For as the heavens are higher than the earth, so are my ways higher than your ways, and my thoughts than your thoughts.
>
> (Isaiah 55:8–9)

In the year 1999, I won the American Lottery Visa which opened a double door for me and my family to come to the United States, God's promised land to us. By the grace of God, I became an ordained minister of the gospel on May 19, 1999, and we arrived in the U.S. exactly one year later on May 19, 2000. To the amazement of everyone, by February 2001, our family of eight had all received visas as American Permanent Residents! We saw the truth from our experience of Proverbs 18:16 which says, "A man's gift maketh room for him, and bringeth him before great men," was made manifest as a true word of God in my life. The gift of the Holy Ghost I had asked for, did not only impact my own life, but also the lives of many men and women as well. As God also promises: "Believe in the LORD your God, so shall ye be established; believe his prophets, so shall ye prosper" (2 Chron. 20:20).

Chapter Twelve

Diligence and Faith Are Rewarded!

In 1981 while I was still in college, I decided to give myself to prayer and fasting. I started on a Friday morning and planned to continue through Sunday evening. I purposed in my heart to have a special time with God. I felt that doing this would enhance my communication with Him and bring it to a higher frequency. Well, my planned step forward worked out in a way I never thought possible. As an executive member of the Christian Union (CU), it was incumbent on me to receive Holy Ghost empowerment as a Christian leader so as to be able to help people solve their spiritual problems. I did not want to be a leader who lacked genuine power to minister effectively to students in need. God rewarded this good intention from my heart by flushing out worms from my body. I had gone through this process as a child when my dad took us through a deworming procedure periodically. At the end of my three days fasting, I went to the toilet and discharged heaps of worms in my bowel movement. Since after that time until today in 2023, I have never again had to deal with an aching stomach as a result of worms. Jehovah Rapha touched me.[21] That day Hebrews 11:6 became clearer to me than ever:

> *But without faith it is impossible to please him: for he that cometh to God must believe that he is, and that he is a rewarder of them that diligently seek him.*
>
> (Hebrews 11:6)

Number one: You must have faith.

Number two: You must seek diligently.

Number three: God is the Rewarder.

The simple formula is this: You + faith + diligence = reward!

During the Nigeria National Labor Strike in 1997, I was led by the Holy Spirit to fast and pray for twenty-one days. In fact, the national strike gave me the opportunity to do this. I would have been unable to do it while working. It was not easy, but the Holy Spirit gave me enormous strength. Throughout this time I drank only water and it was enough. At the end of the fasting period, I was able to hear supernatural voices loud and clear. The Holy Spirit sent me on a special assignment from Owerri to Aba. God told me to go to Aba to the house of Mr. Chukwunyere Nwachukwu and preach the message of salvation to him! It was just as God had spoken to Peter in the Book of Acts! At this juncture, I needed no counselor to give me direction, and there was no time to waste. The message was loud and clear. I boarded a vehicle the same morning and drove straight to Aba. In less than an hour I was in Mr. Nwachukwu's house, which was a distance of about forty miles

---

21   See Exodus 15:26.

from Amakohia in Owerri of Imo state to Aba the industrial and commercial city of Abia state.

When I set foot in Mr. Nwachukwu's house, I skipped every polite protocol, which included the presentation of cola nut and long greetings according to Igbo custom. We sat in the parlor with Amarachi sitting beside her husband Chukwunyere. My message based on John 3:16 was short but powerful. I told them that God sent Jesus to the world so that every man and woman who would confess their sins could receive Jesus as their personal Savior and be able to go to heaven. I finished with John 1:12, which says "But as many as received him, to them gave he power to become the sons of God, even to them that believe on his name." My point was that everyone was created by God, but only those who received Jesus as their personal Savior are the true sons and daughters of God, and only then can they serve God with sincerity of purpose through the power of the Holy Ghost within them.

When I finished my message, Mr. Nwachukwu said, "I know God hears the prayers of preachers of the gospel. Please pray for us that God will bless our marriage with children." I immediately knew that the appointed hour of Holy Ghost manifestation had come. It was time for God to honor His name. We joined hands together (Amarachi, Mr. Nwachukwu, Nelson, the brother-in-law, and myself) and prayed. A month later, Amarachi was pregnant.

Six months later, I traveled to another village from Owerri. Coincidentally, Amarachi came to this village to visit her mother. The moment I saw her, the Holy Ghost gave me a *rhema* word and I told her, "The child you are carrying in your womb is a male child." At the end of the day, we parted to our different destinations.

On Sunday, May 24, 1998, I traveled to Aba again to see my cousin, Brother Samnoble Ebiringa, by the prompting of the Holy Ghost. When I got there, I was climbing the stairway to see Samnoble upstairs when Mr. Nwachukwu beckoned me from behind. On turning, he shared the good news of the baby's birth he had intended to relay to Samnoble. At this juncture, we all stopped and rejoiced together, thanking God for the birth of the new baby boy.

Afterward, Mr. Nwachukwu and I went to the hospital together. On arrival, we gathered and prayed for the child with thanksgiving to God. As you read this testimony, consider the mystery: there is incredible power in fasting and prayer. The Holy Ghost uses you when you surrender your whole life to God without reservation and without compromise. Trust God and obey Him without wavering. God is a rewarder of them that diligently seek Him, and He is a revealer of every secret. Ask and it shall be given you!

Chapter Thirteen

I Believe in Miracles!

Early on Monday, March 10, 1997, I received a revelation from the Lord. In my dream, I saw two coffins in my brother Victor's living room. Victor is an engineer and an elder. One of the coffins I saw was for an adult while the second one was small, for the size of a baby. In my dream, I took the hand of the baby to straighten it and it broke, showing me the real tenderness and fragility of a baby. The moment I woke up, I prayed. After praying, God spoke to me and said, "Go to Owerri and stay in your brother's house for seven days praying and fasting."

I recognized this was an emergency call, and left for Owerri at daybreak, without wasting time. As I alighted from the car along Wetheral road, Owerri in Imo state, I began asking God unusual questions. When I remembered that my brother worked in Orlu, I asked if I should walk or ride a motorcycle to my brother's residence. The answer was, "Walk!" The second question was about direction: "Should I take the Ikenegbu road or the Aladinma road?" He used both, but I would miss him if we took different roads. The response was clear: "The Aladinma road." I went that way. As I was walking along the Aladinma road, I saw my brother driving from the opposite direction. I waved my hand, and he saw me and stopped as if it had been prearranged. I entered the car, telling him that I was on a mission from God and we needed to go back to his house. When we got there, I prayed with the entire family.

Then my brother left for work. I continued in prayer and dry fasting for seven days. God gave me a clear and direct assignment: pray against the spirit of death. One evening I was in a dream when God showed me a two-story building under construction. It was mine! Overwhelmed by this, I started singing, "You are so good, You are so good! Darling Jesus, I worship You. You are so good." I continued singing the song when I woke up from the dream.

(As of today in 2023, I have completed a two-story building as a proof of the goodness of God. God is a rewarder of them that diligently seek Him.) As for my brother and his family, God came through. Saturday, March 1997, his daughter was delivered from the mouth of lion. When she went to the hospital to deliver her baby, little did she know that she could not deliver naturally. After trying her best to no avail, the doctor operated on her to rescue the life of her child and save her life too. It was only by the mercy of God that she and the baby both lived.

The next year (1998) was another milestone in my spiritual journey. As the song says:

'Tis so sweet to trust in Jesus,
Just to take Him at His word,
Just to rest upon His promise;
Just to know, Thus saith the Lord.
Jesus, Jesus, how I trust Him,
How I've proved Him o'er and o'er;
Jesus, Jesus, precious Jesus;

Oh, for grace to trust Him more![22]

One fateful day in August, I received a visitor where I lived with my family. After a short introduction, she told me her mother, our next-door neighbor, asked her to come see me. What seemed strange to me was I had never discussed this daughter with that neighbor that I could remember. It was like when the king of Syria sent Naaman to the king of Israel unannounced in 2 Kings 5:1–7 instead of to Elisha the prophet. We prayed together after she shared her ordeals concerning bearing a child. As I listened, I chose to rely absolutely on God's Word and promises just like David did.

> David said moreover, The LORD that delivered me out of the paw of the lion, and out of the paw of the bear, he will deliver me out of the hand of this Philistine. And Saul said unto David, Go, and the LORD be with thee.
>
> (1 Samuel 17:37)

Afterward I bid her farewell, trusting that the God of Abraham, Isaac, and Jacob would show up. That night, I presented her case to God. In a vision that night, God showed me a frightening wild animal. By this, I concluded that the battle line had been drawn for God's glory. I had not hesitated to ask her about her life before she was married, and she had been transparent and innocent. It turned out that through her mom's religious beliefs, the girl had ignorantly entered into a covenant which needed to be broken before she could conceive and bear children. Thank God for science and technology. She had already been tested, and a scan showed that she had no medical issue.

---

22 "Tis So Sweet to Trust in Jesus" is in the public domain. Its lyrics were written by Louisa M. R. Stead and the music was written by William James Kirkpatrick.

So, the next approach had to be spiritual. We entered into midnight prayer through the inspiration of the Holy Spirit.

The very first day she visited me, God gave me this word: "But upon mount Zion there shall be deliverance, and there shall be holiness; and the house of Jacob shall possess their possessions" (Obad. 1:17). The word of instruction became a signpost in our marathon. With faith in God and patience, we worked on this spiritual assignment for a full year, 365 days.

At the end of the year, God gave me a sign.

One Friday night, my brother, some other men, and I held a vigil. In the early morning of that day I saw a vision of fruitful, plump, and fluted pumpkins in our garden. There were very many of them. After seeing this vision, the Holy Spirit directed me to travel to Portharcourt to witness God's final manifestation of this work He had begun. As a confirmation of the leading of the Holy Spirit, God had Mr. Josiah Nwabugwu, a brother-in-law who was traveling to Portharcourt, make a stop at my brother's house. I hurriedly joined them.

> And it shall come to pass in that day, that his burden shall be taken away from off thy shoulder, and his yoke from off thy neck, and the yoke shall be destroyed because of the anointing.
> (Isaiah 10:27)

Our God is omnipotent, meaning His power is unlimited. He's also everywhere at the same time, or omnipresent, and He knows everything, so He is omniscient. Our amazing God chose that very day to break the yoke of this evil spiritual covenant after 365 days of waiting and interceding for freedom from the shackles of the power of darkness. This woman found her freedom from demons and freedom from marine spirits.

When I arrived in Portharcourt, my friend, who was an oil company engineer, was at home. Often he was at offshore drilling assignments as his schedule took him there regularly, but on the night I arrived, I had a special midnight prayer time with him and his wife. This was an appointed one that completed the year-long cycle which had begun in October 1998 to that night. As you read this testimony, bear in mind that the Mighty Warrior, the Creator of the Universe, has appointed times. Be very sensitive not to miss God's appointed times in your life. God, being outside of time itself, is not subject to time and its seasons. What are you praying for? What are you waiting for? What manifestation of God's are you expecting? Stay in tune with the Spirit of God and wait for it!

> *For the vision is yet for an appointed time, but at the end it shall speak, and not lie: though it tarry, wait for it; because it will surely come, it will not tarry.*
>
> (Habakkuk 2:3)

We prayed together and in the morning, the wife asked, "Is there a Bible passage that says this: 'Upon mount Zion shall be deliverance, and there shall be holiness; and the house of Jacob shall possess their possessions'?" I told her there was and that it was Obadiah 1:17. She said that this *rhema* word had been spoken to her by God before daybreak. No sooner had she finished saying this when the aroma of the Holy Ghost filled the entire room. I remembered that God had given me the same word a year ago when we had prayed together in my house, and I had not shared it with her at the time.

I smiled at the precise way God had confirmed His word, and we sat down and read that verse together. We prayed and thanked the God of heaven, the Lord who had confirmed His word and exalted the horn of His people.[23] From that day forward, she did not menstruate until she gave birth to her first son in June. When a woman is having trouble conceiving, the root of the problem may be either medical or spiritual. It is advisable to know the root of every problem so as to know how to tackle it. To God be the glory for the great things He has done. Jesus said, "If the son therefore shall make you free, ye shall be free indeed" (John 8:36). When the demonic agreement she had ignorantly made when she was young was nullified, she was freed. Once again she was fruitful and gave birth to her first son and two others later on.

God's miracles can use diverse methodology. When God wants to showcase His power, He does not follow protocols. He jumps barriers and obstacles. One day in the year 1999, my niece called me from America, also requesting prayer regarding conception. She was told that she could not conceive because of a fibroid growth in her uterus. The doctor said she had to undergo surgery before she could conceive. We prayed over the phone (my first encounter in the ministry carrying out spiritual warfare on the phone). Miraculously after prayer, she conceived. No obstacle could stop God! God allowed conception to take place in the midst of fibroid growths in the uterus!

The doctor had been skeptical of the possibility of fertilization alone, and did not think there was room for the growth of the fetus. But God in His infinite mercy proved His power of creation, even when it was humanly and scientifically impossible. To the glory of God, there was no abnormality in development and no inhibition in growth. On the fourteenth of October, 2000, her bouncing baby boy arrived.

---

23   See Psalm 148:14, 1 Samuel 2:1, and Luke 1:69.

"I believe in miracles!" said the American evangelist and great woman of God, Kathryn Kulhman. I too believe in miracles—one hundred percent! The God of yesterday is the God of today. "Jesus Christ the same yesterday, and to day, and for ever" (Heb. 13:8). "The God of Abraham, and of Isaac, and of Jacob" (Acts 3:13a) is also the God of Williams Okwuchi Ebiringa! God has been faithful to His Word and promises. God is a man of war. I call Him Mighty Warrior. What are you believing God for?

> But without faith it is impossible to please him: for he that cometh to God must believe that he is, and that he is a rewarder of them that diligently seek him.
>
> (Hebrews 11:6)

The greatest miracle is the miracle of the new birth. Are you born again? Can you recall a particular day when you made a decision to confess your sins and said, "Lord Jesus, please come into my life today. I receive You as my personal Savior"? The moment you make this declaration you become "born again" and something happens.

> That if thou shalt confess with thy mouth the Lord Jesus, and shalt believe in thine heart that God hath raised him from the dead, thou shalt be saved.
>
> (Romans 10:9)

> But as many as received him, to them gave he power to become the sons of God, even to them that believe on his name: which were born, not of blood, nor of the will of the flesh, nor of the will of man, but of God.
>
> (John 1:12–13)

> *Therefore if any man be in Christ, he is a new creature: old things are passed away; behold, all things are become new.*
> (2 Corinthians 5:17)

When you are born again, you receive power from the Spirit of God inside you to live a new life because you are now "a new birth" as explained in that last verse. Congratulations! Your old Adamic sin nature has been overtaken by the nature of Christ. Now that is a true miracle!

Chapter Fourteen

Trusting Prophetic Fulfillment— No Matter What

When I asked for the gift of prophecy, I had no idea it would lead me in these directions. Any time I think of prophecy, I remember how the Bible says that gifts make room for men and elevate them as I have quoted before. I thank God for this noble gift that has granted me access to men in authority, both in the secular and spiritual worlds. Most of all, I enjoy being in partnership with the Holy Ghost.

This reminds me of the words to a song we sing:

When we walk with the Lord in the light of His Word,
What a glory He sheds on our way!
While we do His good will, He abides with us still,
And with all who will trust and obey.[24]

Early in the year 1993, I received a clear message from God that Moshood Kashimawo Olawale Abiola would not rule Nigeria. Chief Abiola was fondly called "M.K.O." He was born in

---

24   "Trust and Obey" was written by John H. Sammis in 1887 and is in public domain.

August of 1937. The name *Kashimawo* means "let us wait and see." Moshood Abiola was his father's twenty-third child but the first of his father's children to survive infancy. The name *Abiola* is of Yoruba origin, meaning "born in honor, wealth."[25] Nigerians loved him, but who was I to challenge God when He says something? When God speaks, it is done.

Whenever I receive a message from God, I deliver it as it was spoken to me. Verbatim. I do not add or subtract even when it's unclear. Some messages do not make sense to me until they manifest. That's just the way it is. There are times I have been disturbed in my spirit while pondering some mystery until it is revealed.

To my greatest surprise, all my friends and relations were excited to vote for Abiola on Election Day, even after I had shared my message with them. I asked them what they saw in this man. What was driving them crazy for Chief Abiola? How did he win their vote? On the morning of the election, we all gathered at the polling ground, waiting for voting to begin. When I discovered that almost everybody I knew had decided to vote for Chief Abiola, my interest in voting died. I was hungry, so I left the polling ground to go home and eat lunch. I love to vote. It is my civic right and duty, but on this particular day, I went home and never went back, and never voted. I felt that my vote would not count, and I believed the message I heard from God. God speaks to His people to give them direction. After all, the Holy Ghost is our GPS.

Surprisingly, on June 12, 1993, the election in which most people had backed Abiola as the new president was annulled, and the country taken over in yet another coup by General Sani

---

25 "Moshood Abiola," Wikipedia (Wikimedia Foundation, January 26, 2023), https://en.wikipedia.org/wiki/Moshood_Abiola.

Abacha. When people started protesting, Chief Abiola maintained that he was the rightful ruler, but he was arrested and put in prison and charged with treason, while his wife was assassinated. He died on the day he was being released, and never became the president of Nigeria.

Although it was tragic, these events confirmed the word of God I had received. A word that flew in the face of public approval and opinion. God knew what would be. Children of God, do not doubt God. If He speaks to you, you should verify the authenticity of any message you receive, and He will confirm His words to you. Once you have done that though, you can stand on whatever He said to you and believe it will come to pass, even when you do not understand how it possibly could.

It is a blessing to be a mouthpiece for God. As the Bible says: "Believe in the LORD your God, so shall ye be established; believe his prophets, so shall ye prosper" (2 Chron. 20:20).

Chapter Fifteen

Can Anything Good Come Out of Nazareth (or Abeokuta)?

My God, the Mighty Warrior, is not a respecter of persons. Your title, age, position, and education are not God's yardstick in showcasing His people. He will always bless those He wants to bless and favor those He wants to favor. It is His prerogative and no one has the power to challenge His will in this.

> *Bless the* LORD, *O my soul: and all that is within me, bless his holy name. Bless the* LORD, *O my soul, and forget not all his benefits.*
>
> (Psalm 103:1–2)

> *Then Peter opened his mouth, and said, Of a truth I perceive that God is no respecter of persons: but in every nation he that feareth him, and worketh righteousness, is accepted with him.*
>
> (Acts 10:34–35)

This God will be my God for ever and ever. In the year 1998, God showed me in a vision that General Olusegun Obasanjo would be the next president of Nigeria. I shared this message to some people I knew. I vividly remember telling my cousin, but he didn't believe me. Very often, a prophet is not without honor except in his own country.

I also told a Nigerian medical doctor, who is a member of the Apostolic Church Owerri in Imo state. He said General Obasanjo had been a weak leader when he was a military leader, and would not perform any magic as a civilian leader. Another time, I was challenged by a Nigeria Youth Service Corps teacher doing his primary assignment at the Ikenegbu Girls' Secondary School in Owerri. He responded with boldness: "Mr. Falaye [another candidate] is our man—our candidate. We, the Yorubas, will not cast our vote for Obasanjo." These were just three testimonies out of the many people I spoke to about this.

Before the end of the year, I conducted a Christian seminar at one of the primary schools in Owerri. At the end of it, I announced that General Olusegun Obasanjo would be our next president. Doing that was an example of faith in action. "Now faith is the substance of things hoped for, the evidence of things not seen" (Heb. 11:1). Election Day was on February 27, 1999, and on May 29, 1999, Chief Obasanjo was sworn in as the president and commander in chief of the Federal Republic of Nigeria.

Chief Obasanjo had been active in the military and politics throughout the civil war and when Abacha took over, he arrested Obasanjo and imprisoned him. While there, he became a born-again Christian with the idea of providentialism strongly influencing his subsequent worldview.[26] This basically

---

26 "Olusegun Obasanjo," Wikipedia (Wikimedia Foundation, January 15, 2023), https://en.wikipedia.org/wiki/Olusegun_Obasanjo.

meant that he accepted that everything that happened on earth was overseen by God and therefore, for the greater good.

Exactly one week after Abacha died on June 8, 1998, under unclear circumstances, Obasanjo was released from the Yola Prison by the administration of General Abdusalami Abubakar. Obasanjo had been sentenced to life three years before "by a military court on trumped-up charges of felony and conspiracy to overthrow the Abacha government, an allegation the former president denied with evidence. Miraculously, God rescued him from Abacha's plot to inject him with viral poison when he was in Yola prison."[27] Just as Joseph was released from prison to become a leader in Pharaoh's palace, and Nelson Mandela of South Africa came out of prison to become president of South Africa, God lifted General Obasanjo out of prison to rule Nigeria for eight years in two terms of a democratically elected government. We have never had another coup.

> *Let no one despise your youth; but be an example to the believers in word, in conduct, in love, in spirit, in faith, in purity.*
> (1 Timothy 4:12 NKJV)

> *Do not quench the spirit. Do not despise prophecies.*
> (1 Thessalonians 5:19–20 NKJV)

Allow the Almighty God to showcase you through the gifts He has given to you. Let the Spirit of God direct and lead you, so you will say what He wants you to say and do what He wants you to do without fear, and regardless of human favor, without

---

27   Gboyega Akinsanmi, "Obasanjo: I Left Prison Broke in 1998," THIS-DAYLIVE Obasanjo I Left Prison Broke in 1998 Comments, 2017, http://www.thisdaylive.com/index.php/2017/07/16/obasanjo-i-left-prison-broke-in-1998/.

doubt and without intimidation of any sort. Always be God's battle-ax.

Chapter Sixteen

Trusting God as My Source

And it shall come to pass afterward
That I will pour out My Spirit on all flesh;
Your sons and your daughters shall prophesy,
Your old men shall dream dreams,
Your young men shall see visions.

(Joel 2:28 NKJV)

God is Waymaker, Miracle Worker, Promise Keeper, Light in the Darkness. He is so awesome. When He equips you with a spiritual gift, He is the Driver of the vehicle. He is the Pilot. He is the Captain of the ship.

We are the children of God, led by the Spirit of God according to Romans 8:14: "For as many as are led by the Spirit of God, these are sons of God" (NKJV). The Almighty God moves and performs His wonders in a mysterious way. He moves you anywhere He pleases and in all kinds of ways to establish His name for His glory. His messages may come to you in a vision, night or day. He may choose to communicate to you in a dream. He may choose to communicate to you in a small, still whisper to your heart, or audibly, or through His written Word. Whichever way, the choice is His.

God may even give you a puzzle which may require you to "go the extra mile" to understand it. As Proverbs 25:2 says:

"It is the glory of God to conceal a matter, but the glory of kings is to search out a matter." One early morning in 1995, I had a vision. I saw a portable radio making a loud and clear announcement. It said, "You are going to be a distributor." I looked around and saw myself in a room full of bread. When I woke up in the morning, I remembered that something had been communicated to me in the dream, but I could not remember any of it. I became worried. I was curious to hear the message.

In my curiosity, I went to my pastor who was also a prophet, the late Pastor Christopher Ugoh. I narrated my dream, and how I received a message but could not remember it anymore. He told me to go home and pray and ask God to relay back the message. I went home and prayed. After prayer, the message came back audibly: "You will be a distributor." I thanked God for repeating His message.

Usually, whenever I had a dream, I forgot it when I woke up; I was not bothered by this because I considered my dreams ordinary. Africans regard dreams as "malaria dreams" meaning that they have no substance and don't mean anything. But in my case, I felt deep in my spirit that my dream was a divine message.

Today, I thank God and rejoice in the Lord that the mercy of God is so great toward me, and that His grace is so awesome and sufficient to me. I have not done much, but God has been supplying all my needs "according to His riches in glory by Christ Jesus" (Phil. 4:19 NKJV). Out of the little I have God has helped me to fulfill His ministry for me.

Sometimes God gives me dreams in which I see myself helping others. At times, it looks as if the source is running dry, but you know what? God has given me this directive, good health, and plenty of energy, so I am able to continue in every task He calls me to do daily, and that is how it should be.

> But thou shalt remember the LORD thy God: for it is he that giveth thee power to get wealth, that he may establish his covenant which he sware unto thy fathers, as it is this day.
>
> (Deuteronomy 8:18)

> For God is not unjust to forget your work and labor of love which you have shown toward His name, in that you have ministered to the saints, and do minister.
>
> (Hebrews 6:10 NKJV)

> And whatever you do, do it heartily, as to the Lord and not to men, knowing that from the Lord you will receive the reward of the inheritance; for you serve the Lord Christ.
>
> (Colossians 3:23–24 NKJV)

Chapter Seventeen

An Emergency Call

The thief cometh not, but for to steal, and to kill, and to destroy: I am come that they might have life, and that they might have it more abundantly.

(John 10:10)

He who sins is of the devil, for the devil has sinned from the beginning. For this purpose the son of God was manifested, that He might destroy the works of the devil.

(1 John 3:8 NKJV)

In his letter, the apostle John brought even greater clarity to the words of Jesus. Since the devil's plans and intention is to destroy lives, his followers and agents follow suit. We must pray we do not fall victim to those plans. James 4:8 tells the children of God to draw nearer and nearer to God and always resist the devil, so he is not able to destroy the precious life God has given you.

In 1996, a noble and prestigious gentleman was the chairman of Obowo L.G.A. in Imo state. The enemies of progress and life struck his life, and he became terribly sick and disoriented. I received a message from God to go and tell him to renounce his allegiance and membership to an occult fraternity into which he had been initiated. In many occult groups, you must take an oath of allegiance. By doing this, you make a covenant with the spirit that controls that group. This gives the deity you owe allegiance to a legal right over your life. When a man belongs to an occult spirit and sees another man of a lesser power occult spirit, the one with the greater power will maneuver the one with less, making him his prey. His intent is to destroy and eliminate him. This kind of power struggle has eaten up students in some of our colleges and universities and caused a lot of bloodshed. Beware of occultism! It is devilish.

Unfortunately, when I spoke to this man, his response was negative. He eventually died without completing his two years in the office. My advice to men and women who search for power is to avoid the native doctors who lead people into these kinds of allegiances. Do not give way to occultism to gain power. The power from the native doctor will fail you. All occult power will fail you. If you are already in any occult, renounce your allegiance to it. Confess your sin to God and accept our Lord Jesus as your personal Savior. Then your life will be secure and led of God: "For you died, and your life is hidden with Christ in God" (Col. 3:3 NKJV).

Do not compromise your faith and sell your hidden power for "a pot of porridge" like Esau did. Your ministry as God's mouthpiece is very delicate. At times your way of life when you are responding to the promptings of the Holy Ghost may appear foolish, even nonsensical, to the eyes of ordinary people. But it's your conviction that matters; it's your driving force. Joshua 1:9 says, "Have not I commanded thee? Be strong and of a good courage; be not afraid, neither be thou dismayed: for the Lord thy God is with thee whithersoever thou goest."

At 5:00 a.m. one morning in 1999, I had a terrible dream. I saw two big trucks squeeze a small car, smashing it in between them. I heard a very loud voice right from the scene of the accident, saying, "Amaonwu!" I woke up with that echo ringing in my ears. Instantly, the Holy Ghost gave me a message to deliver to Elder Felix Amaonwu. He was a member of the Apostolic Church that met in Owerri, Imo state. I did not know him very well, so I did not know where he lived, just where he attended church. You may be somebody or nobody, but Someone knows your house address, sees what you do, knows what you think, hears everything you say, both in the open and in the secret. God has *the best plan ever* for you: "For I know the thoughts that I think toward you, saith the Lord, thoughts of peace, and not of evil, to give you an expected end" (Jer. 29:11).

There was a deacon by the name of Joseph Okoye at the same Apostolic Church that lived close to my house and worked also as a taxi driver. The Holy Spirit led me to his house for assistance. When I got there, he was getting ready to leave. I asked him if he knew where Elder Amaonwu lived and he said yes, so he drove me to Elder Amaonwu's home. The deacon dropped me off, and after exchanging greetings with Elder Amaonwu, he left. As we sat down, I told him my dream and how the Holy Ghost had sent me to him. We joined hands and prayed together.

After we finished praying, he said he always boarded a bus to travel to Port Harcourt from Owerri after the weekend. Today he was running a bit late, and was contemplating driving his car instead. He continued, telling me that since we had prayed, he felt the Holy Ghost was urging him not to do this. God was telling him to avoid this accident. On that same day, Elder Felix Amaonwu eluded the devil's plan to destroy him. God plans a fulfilled life for everyone, while the devil's plan is to cut it short. Hear the promise of God: "With long life will I satisfy him, and shew him my salvation" (Psa. 91:16). Listen to the voice of God and believe the true prophets God sends your way. If you want to travel, and the voice of God tells you to cancel it, just do it. We must all be very attentive to hear God's voice! Thank You, Lord, for caring for us and protecting us in this way.

> *The secret of the LORD is for them that fear him; and he will shew them his covenant.*
>
> (Psalm 25:14)

> *Call unto me, and I will answer thee, and shew thee great and mighty things, which thou knowest not.*
>
> (Jeremiah 33:3)

When you are born again and baptized in the Holy Ghost, you are equipped to see and do extraordinary feats that are beyond the level and frequency of a Christian without the power of the Holy Ghost. Here's the deal: you have to fear God. You must love what He loves and hate what He hates.

> *But as he which hath called you is holy, so be ye holy in all manner of conversation; because it is written, Be ye holy; for I am holy.*
>
> (1 Peter 1:15–16)

> *Thou hast loved righteousness, and hated iniquity; therefore God, even thy God, hath anointed thee with the oil of gladness above thy fellows.*
>
> (Hebrews 1:9)

You must not live a life submitted to these kinds of thoughts: *If you can't beat them, join them,* or, *After all, brother Peter and Sister Sophia do the same, so why not me?*

You may be the next Joseph of your generation, or an Esther or a Daniel. God has a plan for your life. God is looking for you: "And I sought for a man among them, that should make up the hedge, and stand in the gap before me for the land, that I should not destroy it" (Ezek. 22:30). Stand up and be counted.

Chapter Eighteen

Fasting and Prayer

My brethren, count it all joy when ye fall into divers temptations; knowing this, that the trying of your faith worketh patience. But let patience have her perfect work, that ye may be perfect and entire, wanting nothing.

(James 1:2–4)

But he knoweth the way that I take: when he hath tried me, I shall come forth as gold.

(Job 23:10)

I beseech you therefore, brethren, by the mercies of God, that ye present your bodies a living sacrifice, holy, acceptable unto God, which is your reasonable service.

(Romans 12:1)

The trials and temptations you experience in life bring out the *real you*. God's intention and purpose is to refine every Christian as gold is refined by fire. When we are refined, we will daily present our bodies a living sacrifice.

Beloved, let's look at God's *modus operandi* He uses to bring out the *real you*. The *real you* is the Spirit of God He breathes into you.

God is a Spirit: and they that worship him must worship him in spirit and in truth.

(John 4:24)

And the Lord God formed man of the dust of the ground, and breathed into his nostrils the breath of life; and man became a living soul.

(Genesis 2:7)

God breathed into Adam and gave him life. It's through close communication with God that we grow in our faith, and walk in a strong spiritual life. As our trials expose our souls, we find a ready refuge in the Lord. When we give ourselves to prayer, fasting, and the reading of the Word of God, we begin to operate under the supernatural leading of the Holy Spirit according to our gift and the measure of faith we have. He transforms us so that we are changed from one degree of glory to another.[28]

Prayer is simply communicating, talking to God as we would a friend and listening to what He says to us. Reading the Word is often part of prayer too. Sometimes as we read, God makes a verse jump off the page and speaks to us through it. Simply reading Scripture strengthens our hearts and our faith. It's like filling ourselves with treasure.

There are many kinds of fasting. Some fast from 6:00 a.m. to 12 noon every day. Others go from 6:00 a.m. to 3:00 p.m. or 6:00 a.m. to 6:00 p.m., while still others choose night fasting from 6:00 p.m. to 6:00 a.m. Dry fasting is fasting without food or water, and can be done for one day, or three or even seven days at a time. A forty-day fast between the hours of 6:00 a.m. to 6:00 p.m. is another option and can be a dry fast or not. Some fast for twenty-one days and drink only water.

---

28   See 2 Corinthians 3:18.

The best person to guide you in fasting is the Holy Ghost. Just as a medical doctor diagnoses you and gives you a prescription with the appropriate dosage in accordance with your ailment, so the Holy Ghost will diagnose and give you direction for when and how to fast, even the duration of the fast.

Chapter Nineteen

Our Divine Connection

Trust in the Lord with all thine heart; and lean not unto thine own understanding. In all thy ways acknowledge him, and he shall direct thy paths.

(Proverbs 3:5–6)

I will instruct thee and teach thee in the way which thou shalt go: I will guide thee with mine eye.

(Psalm 32:8)

And be not drunk with wine, wherein is excess; but be filled with the Spirit; speaking to yourselves in psalms and hymns and spiritual songs, singing and making melody in your heart to the Lord.

(Ephesians 5:18–19)

For as many as are led by the spirit of God, they are the sons of God.

(Romans 8:14)

Howbeit when he, the Spirit of truth, is come, he will guide you into all truth: for he shall not speak of himself; but whatsoever he shall hear, that shall he speak: and he will shew you things to come.

(John 16:13)

Connection plays a vital role in one's life. We are meant to live connected to other people, but most of all, we are meant to live connected to God through His Holy Spirit. The Holy Spirit connects you to your destiny. He is your spiritual mentor for spiritual advancement. The Holy Spirit connects you to financial breakthrough.

The internet is a wonderful and powerful tool that the whole world depends on today for connection. One day my daughter told me that the Spirit of God was telling her to relocate and join another company. I advised her to ask God for direction and not to resign her present job until she found a new one. As she was waiting and trusting God for direction, a friend connected her to another friend who connected her to a big firm through the internet. Today she is comfortably employed and living where she wanted to live in the U.S.

One early morning, I was dreaming and saw myself in an office. In that office, I received an unusual favor. The moment I woke up, the Spirit of God told me to travel to the Zonal School Board Okigwe to meet the director of education. I never planned to embark on this journey, but the Spirit of God compelled me. I sensed that it was urgent. I dressed and told my brother that I was traveling to the School Board Okigwe. He was surprised by this sudden decision to travel. I left Owerri to go to Okigwe (both are in Imo state in Nigeria).

No sooner had I arrived at the office when the director, the late Chief John Kafor asked me to apply to be posted to the Community Secondary School, Ikenanzizi, also in Imo state. I hadn't even had a chance to tell him why I had come, and he had not followed any of our usual protocol either! It turned out that the Mathematics/Chemistry teacher had just tendered his resignation. They wanted me to fill the vacancy immediately. I became the senior Mathematics/Chemistry teacher there for the next nine years. I was not only a teacher, but also served as a Christian counselor and mentor to students. It is sweet to walk and work in partnership with the Holy Ghost. It is the inheritance of every believer to live in daily connection with Him. To God be the glory!

About the Author

The Reverend Williams Okwuchi Ebiringa was born in Umuariam in Imo state, Nigeria. He is from the lineage of Eri, the son of Gad, one of the sons of Jacob. Born in 1953, Williams and his wife, Bernice, have six children: Chioma, Oluomchi, Ezeoma, Ideeze, David, and Jimaimah. They have two sons-in-law: Noble and Samuel and many grandchildren.

A mathematics teacher, a Christian counselor, a prophet, and a psalmist, Williams graduated from Word of Faith Bible Institute of the Winner's Chapel Owerri, Imo state. He was a student of the Center for Biblical Counseling and a member of American Association of Christian Counselors (AACC). While in Obowo, Nigeria, he served in the Apostolic Church as a Sunday school teacher and Sunday school superintendent. He was also a school representative for the Scripture Union for some secondary schools. As an itinerant evangelist, he has touched many souls, and seen the Holy Ghost deliver them from their spiritual bondages and limitations.

In the United States, he served in the Washington, D.C., chapter of the African Christian Fellowship as Outreach Director and Bible Study Director. His heartbeat is for evangelism, and he continues to reach out to people as the Holy Spirit directs him today.

If You Enjoyed This Book, Will You Help Me Spread the Word?

There are several ways you can help me get the word out about the message of this book...

- Post a 5-Star review on Amazon.
- Write about the book on your Facebook, Twitter, Instagram, LinkedIn—any social media you regularly use!
- If you blog, consider referencing the book, or publishing an excerpt from the book with a link back to my website. You have my permission to do this if you provide proper credit and backlinks.
- Recommend the book to friends—word-of-mouth is still the most effective form of advertising.

www.ingramcontent.com/pod-product-compliance
Lightning Source LLC
Chambersburg PA
CBHW051325120626
46547CB00015B/2397